Contents

History in Perspective	4
Key Events: What Happened When	6
Key People: Who's Who	8
Key Location: The Coffin Family's House	10
A Nation Divided	12
Life Under Slavery	14
The Underground Railroad is Born	16
Stealthy Stationmasters	18
Courageous Conductors	20
Journey to Freedom	22
Working Undercover	26
Famous Escapes	28
Risk of Capture	30
Fight for Abolition	32
Growing Desperate	34
The Railroad's Impact	36
Lessons from History	38
Uncovering the Truth	40
Vocabulary Builder: Secret Journeys	42
Glossary	44
Index	46

Words in **bold** are explained in the glossary on page 44.

History in Perspective

For over four **decades**, more than 100,000 **enslaved** Black American individuals made their way to independence. They were known as **freedom seekers**. With the help of some brave people, they used a system of escape known as the Underground Railroad. This created a network of **activists** fighting for **abolition**.

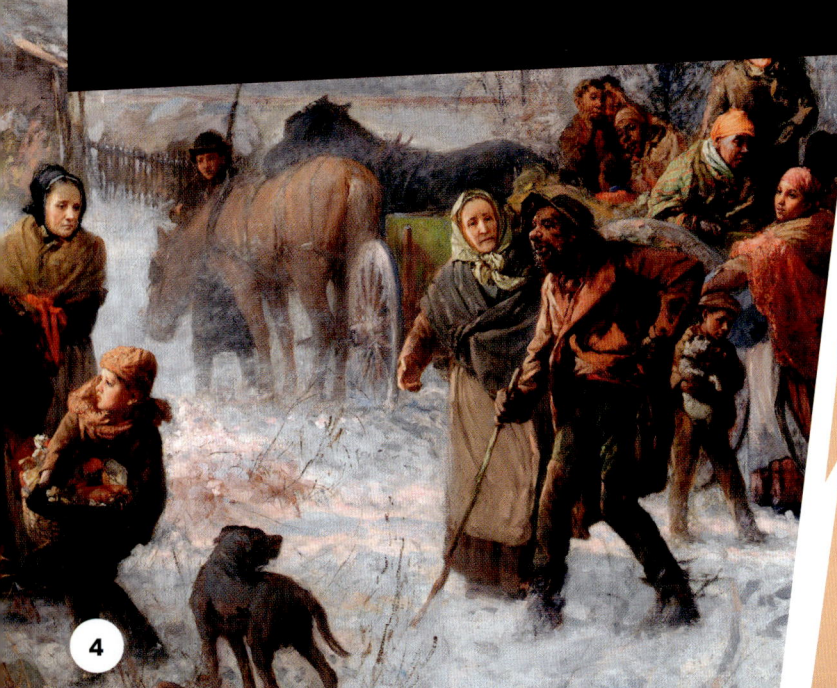

Freedom seekers did not use an actual railway. They mostly travelled on foot during the night.

Where and when?

Many Black American people were enslaved in the southern United States. In these states, owning workers and treating them poorly was common. From 1820 to 1860, many enslaved Black American people ran away to find freedom on their own in the northern states. Over time, more white people began to see that **slavery** was wrong. They started to find ways to help enslaved individuals escape.

DK SUPER History

UNDERGROUND RAILROAD

Learn all about the legendary secret network that helped liberate enslaved people in America during the 18th and 19th centuries

PRODUCED FOR DK BY
Editorial Just Content Limited
Design Studio Noel

Author Lisa Bolt Simmons

Senior Editor Ankita Awasthi Tröger
Editor Hattie Hansford
Senior Art Editor Gilda Pacitti
Graphic Story Illustrator Matt Garbutt
Managing Editor Carine Tracanelli
Managing Art Editor Sarah Corcoran
Pre-Production Coordinator Shanker Prasad
Pre-Production Designer Jaypal Chauhan
Production Controller Rebecca Parton
Publisher Sarah Forbes
Managing Director, Learning Hilary Fine

First published in Great Britain in 2026 by
Dorling Kindersley Limited
20 Vauxhall Bridge Road,
London SW1V 2SA

The authorised representative in the EEA is
Dorling Kindersley Verlag GmbH. Arnulfstr. 124,
80636 Munich, Germany

Copyright © 2026 Dorling Kindersley Limited
A Penguin Random House Company
10 9 8 7 6 5 4 3 2 1
001–350116–Feb/2026

All rights reserved.
No part of this publication may be reproduced, stored in or
introduced into a retrieval system, or transmitted, in any form,
or by any means (electronic, mechanical, photocopying,
recording, or otherwise), without the prior written permission
of the copyright owner.

No part of this publication may be used or reproduced in
any manner for the purpose of training artificial intelligence
technologies or systems. In accordance with Article 4(3)
of the DSM Directive 2019/790, DK expressly reserves this
work from the text and data mining exception.

A CIP catalogue record for this book
is available from the British Library.
ISBN: 978-0-2417-4474-1

Printed and bound in China

www.dk.com

This book was made with Forest Stewardship Council™ certified paper – one small step in DK's commitment to a sustainable future. Learn more at www.dk.com/uk/information/sustainability

The Underground Railroad helped people fleeing slavery get from one point to another on their journey to freedom in the North. Not all white people believed in enslaving other human beings. Some families helped enslaved people. Many felt that slavery was a sin. Some people even believed that God would **condemn** those who enslaved others.

Think about it

We can learn about the Underground Railroad from newspapers, journals, diaries and other written documents from the time. Most of these first-hand **sources** were written by white people. Why do you think that gives a limited view of what happened?

Who was involved?

People who helped freedom seekers went by different code words, such as "conductors", "stationmasters" or "engineers". These code words kept their identities secret. Free Black American people often helped enslaved people escape. Because of the dangers involved, most of the helpers will never be known. Many different elements contributed to the Underground Railroad cause, including **abolitionist** newspapers, speeches, books and sometimes even violence.

Different perspectives

Different groups in society may have deeply contrasting experiences of events. Official records of the past often only present one side of the story. This means that they can't reflect the experiences of everyone affected. To understand what happened, it is important that we look at events from more than one point of view.

Key Events
WHAT HAPPENED WHEN

The fight against slavery grew stronger over the course of the 19th century. More and more white people joined the cause, both in secret and publicly. The Underground Railroad shows how Black American people led the way in seeking freedom and fighting for their rights. The movement was very important in helping many escape enslavement.

1826

OCTOBER

Levi Coffin settles in Newport, Indiana (now known as Fountain City). He and his family build a home that becomes a stop on three routes of the Underground Railroad.

1837

7 NOVEMBER

Elijah Lovejoy, an abolitionist printer, is murdered by a pro-slavery mob. This inspires John Brown to become an abolitionist.

1831

1 JANUARY

William Lloyd Garrison publishes the first issue of his newspaper, *The Liberator*. It openly criticises slavery. Frederick Douglass, a formerly enslaved man, meets with Garrison to tell his story.

1833

DECEMBER

Garrison cofounds the American Anti-Slavery Society. The society encourages the **boycott** of cotton and other items produced by enslaved people. It also encourages **civil disobedience**.

1850

18 SEPTEMBER

The **Fugitive** Slave Act is passed by **Congress**. It gives people the right to capture runaways without **due process** or court proceedings. The act forbids anyone from helping fugitives or blocking **bounty hunters** from capturing them.

1860

From 1850 to 1860, the famous abolitionist Harriet Tubman travels back and forth 19 times from the South to the North. She leads more than 300 enslaved people to freedom.

1865

9 APRIL

Confederate Army General Robert E Lee surrenders to Union Army General Ulysses S Grant. This is considered the beginning of the end of the Civil War. The last Confederate troops later surrender on 6 November, putting an end to the fighting.

1861

12 APRIL

The Confederate States Army fires upon Fort Sumter, South Carolina, marking the start of the Civil War. Starting in 1860, several southern states **secede** from the **Union** because they believe in the institution of slavery.

1865

DECEMBER

Garrison publishes his final issue of *The Liberator*. Georgia becomes the last state needed to **ratify** the Thirteenth **Amendment**. This makes slavery officially illegal in the United States. The Thirteenth Amendment forms part of the US **Constitution**.

Key People
WHO'S WHO

The Underground Railroad helped more than 100,000 enslaved Black American people find freedom in the North. Here are some of the key people in this story.

Abolitionists

William Lloyd Garrison
A strong **advocate** for abolition and non-violence. He founded the weekly abolitionist newspaper *The Liberator*, which ran for more than 30 years.

Frederick Douglass
A formerly enslaved man who wrote a best-selling autobiography, and published a newspaper called *The North Star*.

Harriet Tubman
Tubman was enslaved as a child but escaped to freedom in 1849. She helped other enslaved people find freedom.

Sojourner Truth
Truth was born free but was enslaved and forced into **hard labour.** She ran away to became one of the most famous abolitionists of the time.

John Brown
As a **Calvinist**, Brown believed all people should be treated equally. He also thought violence could be justified if it would end slavery.

Sojourner Truth

Conductors and stationmasters

Thomas Garrett
A stationmaster based for 40 years on the eastern route of the Underground Railroad.

Jermain Loguen
Loguen became famous for helping many enslaved Black American people escape to freedom in Syracuse, New York.

Levi and Catharine Coffin
A married **Quaker** couple. The Coffins hid freedom seekers in their house in what is now Fountain City, Indiana.

Leonard Grimes
A cab driver in Washington, DC. Grimes helped runaways escape by hiding them in his carriage. In 1839, Grimes was caught and sentenced to two years of hard labour.

William Whipper
A lumberyard owner. Whipper helped freedom seekers escape to Canada after the passage of the Fugitive Slave Act.

Leonard Grimes

Escaped and free

Tice Davids
Davids escaped enslavement in Kentucky in 1831 by swimming across the Ohio River. He was followed by his enslaver in a boat. Little is known of his fate.

Henry "Box" Brown
Enslaved in Virginia, Brown escaped by hiding in a box and shipping himself to the Philadelphia Anti-Slavery Society office.

William and Ellen Craft
A married couple who disguised themselves to travel to Philadelphia, Pennsylvania, by steamboat and train.

Solomon Northup
A free man from New York who was kidnapped and sold into slavery in 1841. He found freedom over 10 years later.

Ellen Craft

William Craft

Key Location
THE COFFIN FAMILY'S HOUSE

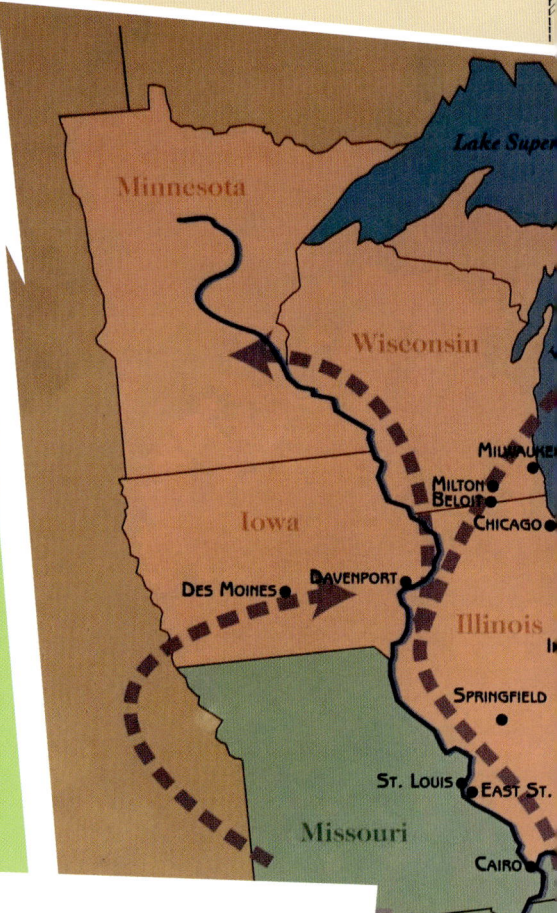

Levi and Catharine Coffin opposed slavery. They were determined to do what they could to help enslaved people who were trying to escape. In 1826, they moved to Fountain City, Indiana, which was then known as Newport. Their house was built in 1839 with special features to help freedom seekers. This two-storey, eight-room house was home to the Coffins from 1839 to 1847. They lived there with their family. They also let freedom seekers travelling to Canada use it as a hiding place. It was such an important stopping point that it became known as the Grand Central Station of the Underground Railroad.

It is estimated that more than 1,000 freedom seekers used the house as a safe haven as they made their way to Canada.

CLEVER DESIGN

The house was designed with plenty of places to hide, including a bedroom with a small door. The door was usually hidden from view by furniture and led to a secret space. The basement had a second kitchen and an indoor well.

The indoor well was fed by a fresh spring. It may have been used to supply freedom seekers with water without neighbours wondering why the Coffins were using so much water.

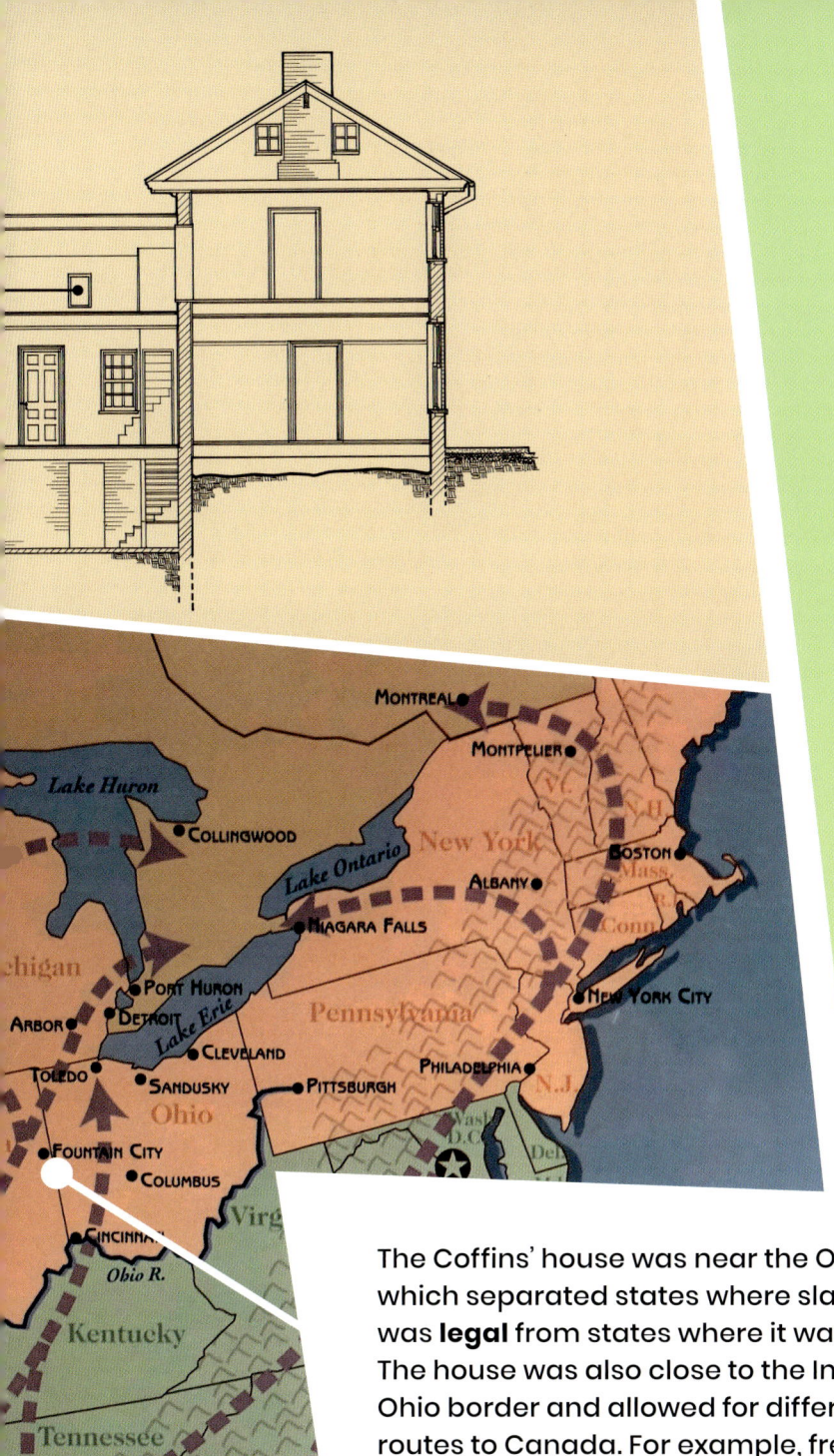

Today, the Coffin family's house is a museum that people can visit to learn more about the Underground Railroad.

The Coffins' house was near the Ohio River, which separated states where slavery was **legal** from states where it was not. The house was also close to the Indiana–Ohio border and allowed for different routes to Canada. For example, freedom seekers could travel through Ohio and Lake Erie or through Michigan.

This map shows the main Underground Railroad routes as purple dashed arrows. These run from states shown in green that allowed slavery to those where it was illegal in orange. The state names and boundaries are given as they were during the period of the Underground Railroad.

A Nation Divided

When the constitution of the US was signed in 1787, it described freedom as a blessing. However, this freedom did not extend to the millions of enslaved people who were forced to work without pay, mostly in the South.

This map is from 1857, before the Civil War. The states shown with no shading were free. Those with darkest shading allowed enslavement. The other states had not yet entered the Union and were undecided on whether they would allow enslavement or be free states.

MISSOURI COMPROMISE

By 1820 there was an equal number of states that did or did not allow slavery. Slavery was **outlawed** in Maine, so when it asked to join the Union people worried that free states would have more power. The US Congress allowed Missouri to join as a state where slavery was legal as a compromise. They thought it would keep things fair and balanced and stop arguments between the North and the South about slavery.

ANTI-SLAVERY SOCIETIES

The New England Anti-Slavery Society was formed in 1831. Within five years, it had local groups in Ohio, Massachusetts and New York. In 1833, the American Anti-Slavery Society was founded. Just five years later, it had almost 250,000 members. Even though its members sometimes disagreed about politics and religion, they worked together to convince the public that slavery was wrong. They continued their work for many years, making more white people accept that slavery was wrong and cruel.

William Lloyd Garrison founded the New England Anti-Slavery Society and co-founded the American Anti-Slavery Society. Garrison believed in convincing people that slavery was wrong in non-violent ways. He spoke and wrote about why everyone should be free.

Frederick Douglass founded an anti-slavery newspaper called *The North Star* that was published from 1847 to 1851. He later edited two other newspapers.

BLACK ABOLITIONISTS

Although they had white **allies**, Black abolitionists and formerly enslaved people published their own newspapers. They also organised meetings. These groups played a huge role in the abolitionist movement.

Fascinating fact

Douglass was the most photographed American person of the 19th century. Over 160 portraits were taken of him. He believed photography was a powerful tool that could change views of Black American people.

Samuel Cornish was a **minister** and abolitionist. He believed slavery was wrong. Alongside John Brown Russwurm, Cornish published a newspaper called *Freedom's Journal*. In it, they hoped to tell the stories of Black American people free from the **bias** of white-owned newspapers.

Life Under Slavery

Enslaved individuals were considered to be property by their enslavers. On **plantations**, everyone had to work, even young children, elderly people and those who were sick or hurt. Most enslaved people worked from dawn to dusk, six days a week. During the planting and harvesting seasons, they had to work 15 to 16 hours a day. At first, tobacco plantations were the most common. But during the 19th century, cotton became the most valuable **crop**.

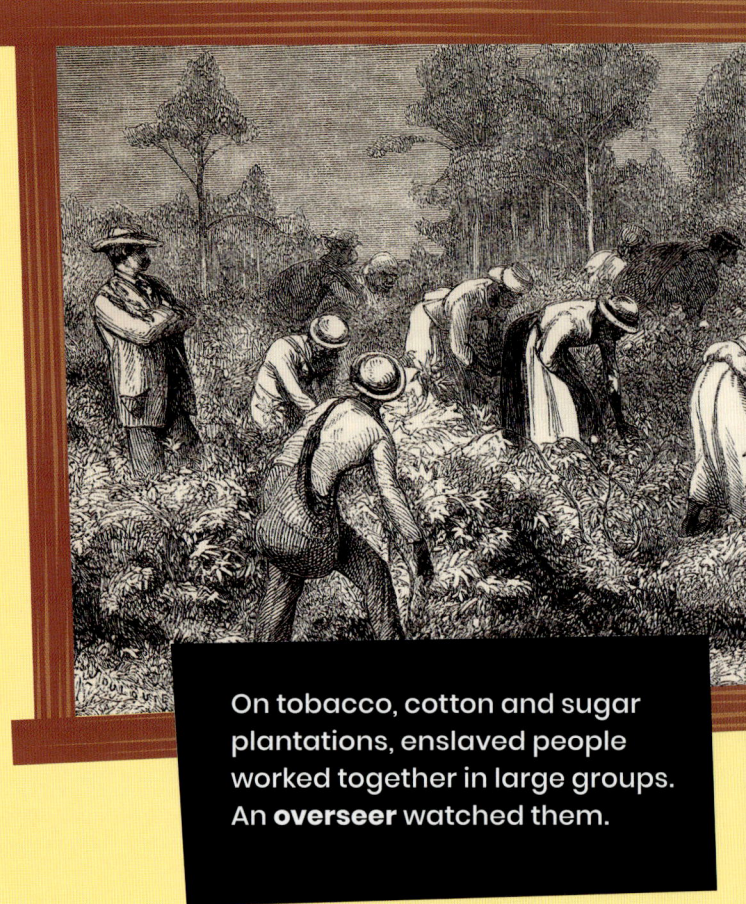

On tobacco, cotton and sugar plantations, enslaved people worked together in large groups. An **overseer** watched them.

HOUSEHOLD LABOUR

Enslaved Black American people also worked in the big houses on the plantations. They cleaned, cooked, made beds, took care of the children, kept fires going and carried out other household chores. Older or disabled enslaved people made clothes, spun cotton and helped in the kitchen.

Enslaved Black American people were often sold at **auctions**. Since the marriages of enslaved people were not legally recognised, an enslaver could sell any family member at an auction and split up the family.

BRUTAL PUNISHMENT

Physical punishment was a fundamental part of the slavery system. Enslavers were often very cruel and used whipping as discipline. In extreme cases, chains and shackles were used for those who had tried to escape.

Think about it

The **mortality rate** was high for enslaved infants. About half died during their first year. The life expectancy of an enslaved person was only 21 years old. Why do you think this was?

INCREASED DEMAND

In 1793, an American engineer named Eli Whitney invented a machine known as the cotton gin. It removed seeds from the cotton fibre, making farming quicker and more **profitable**. As a result, more farmers wanted to grow cotton. This meant more enslaved people were wanted to work on the plantations.

Instead of reducing slavery, the cotton gin made it worse. Cotton plantation owners wanted more enslaved people to work in their fields.

REBELLIONS

Some enslaved Black American people fought for their freedom. Nat Turner led a group of other enslaved people to rebel against their enslavers. First, they killed Turner's enslaver and his family. By the time the rebellion had been stopped, they had killed 55 to 65 people.

Turner was caught two months after the rebellion ended. The event caused white politicians to pass stricter laws that further limited what enslaved people could do. Turner and many of his followers were later **executed**.

The Underground Railroad is Born

Many enslaved Black American people tried to escape their lives of **captivity**. Some wanted to visit family and friends for a short period, while others hoped to find freedom forever. But running away was very dangerous. This is why the secret system of the Underground Railroad was created to help them.

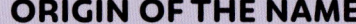

Images like this engraving of an enslaved Black American man running away were used on posters that offered rewards for the capture and return of freedom seekers.

People used whatever methods of travel they could to escape enslavement. This included wagons, horses, boats and even trains.

ORIGIN OF THE NAME

No one knows for certain where the term "Underground Railroad" comes from. In 1831, Tice Davids fled from his enslaver's home and swam across the Ohio River while his enslaver chased after him in a boat. Once Davids reached the riverbank, he disappeared. It is claimed that his enslaver said that Davids "must have gone off on an underground road". No sources confirm if this is true, but people did start to use the phrase after this.

Isaac Hopper was a **liberal** Quaker and abolitionist. He helped the Underground Railroad in Philadelphia, Pennsylvania and New York. By 1834, Hopper was well-known across the country, especially in New York, for housing freedom seekers.

QUAKERS

Quakers believed that slavery was evil. It was not allowed in their religion. Quakers who lived along the Underground Railroad did not turn freedom seekers away or return them to their enslavers.

A survey marker stone from the 18th century. It shows the most southern point of the Mason–Dixon line.

MASON–DIXON LINE

Between 1763 and 1767, two English surveyors named Charles Mason and Jeremiah Dixon established the boundary between the major East Coast states of Pennsylvania and Maryland. This boundary was known as the Mason–Dixon Line. Before the Civil War, this line was the border between the South, where Black American people were enslaved, and the North, where they were free.

SECRET NETWORK

It is not possible to trace the exact routes that runaways took, but we know most freedom seekers fled to the North. At first, they did so alone. But in time, many free Black American people in the North started to help. They formed groups to give food and shelter to freedom seekers, help them find work and protect them from getting caught. These groups were known as **vigilance** committees.

Stealthy Stationmasters

Stationmasters were people who helped freedom seekers run away. They provided hiding places in their houses, or in buildings such as barns and warehouses. As more freedom seekers fled north, the Underground Railroad grew. More stationmasters were needed on the routes. These brave people played an important role in helping Black American people escape enslavement.

Thomas Garrett was a stationmaster on the eastern route of the Underground Railroad for 40 years. There was once a $10,000 bounty for his capture (nearly £290,000 in today's money).

Levi and Catharine Coffin's house in Indiana was positioned where three Underground Railroad routes met. They helped thousands of freedom seekers.

Presbyterian minister Reverend John Rankin and his wife Jean were stationmasters at their home in Ohio. They lived close to the Ohio River, which separated the free state of Kentucky from Ohio where slavery was still allowed.

Jermain Loguen was one of the most active stationmasters in the country.

NEW YORK STATIONMASTERS

The state of New York bordered free states and Canada, making it an important destination for many freedom seekers. In Syracuse, Jermain Loguen was a preacher and activist who is thought to have helped more than 1,500 Black American people find freedom.

In New York City, David Ruggles was the first Black bookshop owner in the United States. He sold abolitionist books, newspapers and **pamphlets**, and also helped freedom seekers. His business was burned down twice, and he was attacked several times.

Stephen Myers helped hundreds of freedom seekers in Albany, New York. Stephen and his wife Harriet helped others for nearly 30 years and their house was the office of the Vigilance Committee of Albany.

This image is part of a cartoon by Edward Williams Clay called *The Disappointed Abolitionists*. The man portrayed in the middle is David Ruggles.

Stephen Myers was born enslaved but gained his freedom at the age of 18.

Courageous Conductors

As the struggle against slavery continued, courageous people became conductors on the Underground Railroad. Conductors helped move people from place to place. They risked their lives to help freedom seekers. Using local knowledge and skills, they guided freedom seekers along dangerous routes, often travelling at night. They provided transportation, shelter and support.

Before becoming a minister, Leonard Grimes was an Underground Railroad conductor. He was a **hackman** in Washington, DC. It was the perfect cover to help runaways, as they would ride in his carriage on their way to freedom.

DANGEROUS WORK

Harriet Tubman was a famous Black American abolitionist, born around 1820 in Maryland. She was enslaved as a child but escaped to freedom in 1849. Instead of staying safe, Tubman returned to the South many times to help others escape slavery on the Underground Railroad.

Think about it

What skills would have been important for conductors?

RISK-TAKER

John P Parker was sold and separated from his mother at the age of 8. He was forced to walk in chains from Virginia to Alabama in a line of enslaved people. He eventually bought his freedom and built a house in Ohio, where he worked and started a family. As a conductor, he took great risks, going to farms in Kentucky at night and bringing hundreds of freedom seekers to safety. Being a conductor was especially dangerous for Parker because bounty hunters knew who he was.

INTERNATIONAL CONDUCTOR

William Whipper was a successful business owner. He was the son of an enslaved Black woman and her white enslaver. Whipper first became a conductor in Pennsylvania. He helped hundreds of freedom seekers.

Whipper's family wanted him to move to Canada after people supporting slavery tried to burn down his business several times. Instead, he stayed in the United States, visiting his warehouse in Canada by rail. The railway carriages contained secret compartments that freedom seekers hid in, allowing them to escape to Canada.

TRAGEDY TO TRIUMPH

Laura Smith Haviland was a Quaker who lost her husband, parents, sister and youngest child to illness. Through her grief, she occupied herself with the abolitionist movement. Haviland helped freedom seekers move through Michigan, Indiana and Ohio as they made their way to Canada. In this photograph she is holding some objects used to restrain enslaved people to raise awareness of the cruelty involved.

Journey to Freedom

Harriet Tubman
Enslaved woman and abolitionist

John Tubman
Harriet's husband

Ben Ross
One of Harriet's younger brothers

Henry Ross
Another of Harriet's younger brothers

William Still
A business owner and leading abolitionist

Born in 1822, Harriet Tubman was originally named Araminta Ross, or Minty. She grew up enslaved in Dorchester County, Maryland.

Araminta was often separated from her family as they all worked from a very young age.

Araminta learned from visiting sailors about a network helping enslaved people escape.

"Travel north across the Mason-Dixon line and Black people are free."

She married John Tubman, a free Black man, and changed her name to Harriet Tubman.

John did not share Harriet's dream.

"I want to take the chance to be free!"

"I am not enslaved. I don't need to risk my life to help you escape."

Working Undercover

The work of the Underground Railroad had to be done **undercover**. People caught helping freedom seekers suffered brutal physical punishments, imprisonment and even execution.

Harriet Tubman

SECRET COMMUNICATION

Harriet Tubman used secret communication methods to send messages to freedom seekers. She sang certain songs, **mimicked** an owl and posted coded letters. Different songs, calls or messages signalled it was time for runaways to keep moving or stay hidden.

CAREFUL PLANNING

Tubman risked her own life to help freedom seekers. She was very careful about how she travelled as she often went out at night. She carried a gun to protect herself and the people she was helping. Tubman knew she could be captured or even killed, but she kept going back to help more people escape.

Code words	Meaning
bundles of wood or parcels	incoming freedom seekers
French leave	sudden departure
patter roller	hunter of freedom seekers
passengers, cargo, freight or baggage	freedom seekers
tickets	freedom seekers on trains
freedom trails	routes
terminal, heaven or promised land	northern free states and Canada

These are some of the code words Tubman used in her messages.

CODED QUILTS

Quilts have knots, shapes and other symbols. Some historians believe these might have helped freedom seekers communicate their travel plans and send other coded messages.

This quilt was made by Harriet Powers, a woman born enslaved in Georgia who later became free. Powers' quilts are now considered important pieces of American folk art.

Fascinating fact

Tubman used two songs to communicate with freedom seekers on the Underground Railroad. She would change the song speed so that runaways would know if it was safe to come out of hiding or if they should stay hidden.

"FOREVER FREE"

As a child, Frederick Douglass learned the alphabet from Sophia Auld, one of his enslavers. Auld's husband would not allow her to continue teaching Douglass, because it was illegal. So Douglass taught himself to read and write. In his teens, Douglass was sent to work as a farmhand under different enslavers. During this time, he taught other enslaved people to read and write. Douglass tried many times to escape to freedom before succeeding in 1838. Douglass famously wrote, "Once you learn to read, you will be forever free" (Douglass, 1845).

Frederick Douglass escaped by disguising himself as a sailor.

Famous Escapes

It took desperate acts for enslaved Black American people to reach freedom. Yet when they were finally free, sometimes they were still not safe. The threat of bounty hunters was never far away. Some formerly enslaved people fled to Canada, England and other countries to keep their freedom.

HENRY "BOX" BROWN

Henry Brown was born enslaved in Virginia. At 1.7 m (5 ft 8 in), he was a tall man. To escape to freedom, he convinced Samuel A Smith, a white shoemaker, to ship him to Pennsylvania in a box that was 1 m (3 ft) long, 0.8 m (2 ft 6 in) deep and 0.6 m (2 ft) wide. The box had tiny holes so that Brown could breathe, and he took a supply of water and biscuits with him. The box was marked "dry goods" and "this side up with care". But Brown spent hours upside down and almost died.

The box arrived at the Philadelphia Anti-Slavery Society office, where four people opened it. Brown stood up and shook their hands. He had spent 27 hours inside, but finally, he was free.

Ellen Craft in disguise, dressed as a white male enslaver.

HIDING IN PLAIN SIGHT

William and Ellen Craft were enslaved in Georgia by different enslavers. William convinced his wife, who had lighter skin, to dress up as his white male enslaver. Ellen could not write, so she pretended to have a broken arm. This way, no one would ask her to sign anything. William acted as her enslaved companion. On 21 December 1848, the Crafts set out on a four-day journey. They stayed at the best hotel in Charleston, South Carolina, and had breakfast with a steamboat captain. They rode first class on trains. When they arrived in Philadelphia, they were free.

William Craft   Ellen Craft

THE LIBERTY LINE

In 1844, a Chicago newspaper called the *Western Citizen* published an advert for the Liberty Line. In reality, it was a reference to the Underground Railroad.

Written by Reverend John Cross, the advert invited those seeking better lives to use the route.

Two years after their escape, the Fugitive Slave Act of 1850 threatened the Crafts' freedom. They left for England, where they lived for 20 years.

Think about it ??

Why do you think the *Western Citizen* editors printed the Liberty Line advert?

Risk of Capture

This image shows a freedom seeker being captured by a bounty hunter. The Fugitive Slave Act of 1850 encouraged ordinary citizens to help capture escaped enslaved people. People found helping a fugitive could be fined $500. That is slightly more than £15,000 in today's money.

When the US Constitution was written, Article Four laid out how the relationships between the states would work. It also included what is known as the Fugitive Slave **Clause**. This clause stated that all enslaved people who escaped to another state must be returned to their enslaver. Later, the Fugitive Slave Acts of 1793 and 1850 were passed to try and force all states to return runaways.

AN EVEN GREATER THREAT

The first federal Fugitive Slave Act was signed in 1793. This law guaranteed that enslavers could recover any runaways, as outlined in Article Four. But in 1850, a second Fugitive Slave Act went even further. It gave bounty hunters the right to search for suspected runaways and return them to their home state.

The act made it hard for escaped enslaved people to live safely in the northern states, as it encouraged everyone to help catch freedom seekers. This meant that many people fleeing enslavement tried to reach Canada to secure their freedom. But even in Canada, life was not easy. Black people still faced unfair treatment. Many had trouble finding jobs and were often kept separate from white people.

KIDNAPPED

Solomon Northup was a free Black man living in New York. In 1841, he was kidnapped and sold into slavery. On the ship Orleans, from Richmond, Virginia, to New Orleans, Louisiana, he was given the name Plat Hamilton. He worked on a cotton plantation before he was rescued in 1853. Northup published his autobiography, *Twelve Years a Slave*. This was later made into a film.

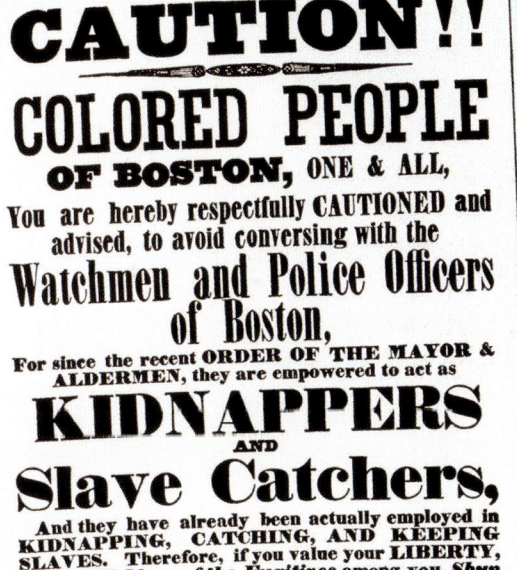

This poster was published in Boston, Massachusetts, around 1850. It warns free Black American people about the risks of being kidnapped. Kidnappers would abduct Black American people and **smuggle** them into the South, where they could sell them into slavery.

This shipper's **manifest** is from the ship Orleans. It lists details about individuals on board the ship such as name, age, sex, race and height. On line 33, it lists Northup under the name of Plat Hamilton.

After 12 years of enslavement, Northup was rescued and reunited with his family.

Fight for Abolition

The aim of the abolitionists was to secure freedom for all enslaved people. Abolitionists strongly believed that slavery was wrong and worked hard to end it. They organised rallies, wrote articles and circulated **petitions** to raise awareness about the evils of slavery. They campaigned in the US and overseas.

Maria Weston Chapman founded the Boston Female Anti-Slavery Society in 1833. The group raised awareness and money to help fight slavery.

Although Truth never learned to read or write, she **dictated** her autobiography, delivered a famous speech about women's rights and was invited to meet President Abraham Lincoln.

PREACHING THE TRUTH

Sojourner Truth (named Isabella Baumfree at birth) was born in New York in 1797. She was born enslaved, and was bought and sold four times before the age of 30. While enslaved, she was forced to do hard labour and suffered brutal punishment. After she had children, Truth ran away to an abolitionist family. They bought her freedom for $20. In 1828, she moved to New York City and worked for a local minister. She believed that preaching the truth was her calling. So, in 1843, she renamed herself Sojourner Truth.

ABOLITIONIST TRAVELLER

Abby Kelley Foster spent more than 20 years travelling the country in the name of **social justice**. She was a national **delegate** in the Anti-Slavery Convention of American Women in 1837. In the 1850s, she worked for the American Anti-Slavery Society.

Foster believed that the inequalities experienced by Black American people and women were closely linked. She argued that both groups deserved the same rights and opportunities in society.

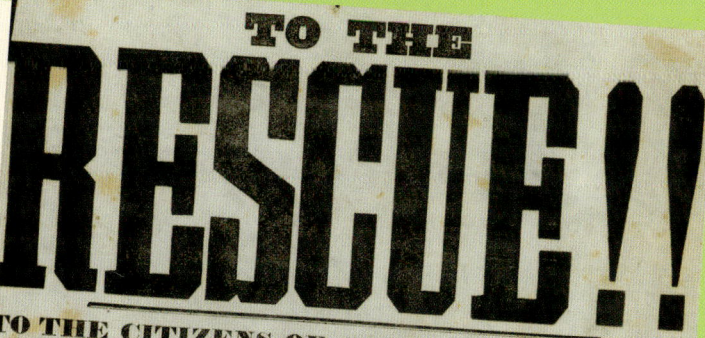

Fascinating fact

Gerrit Smith was a wealthy abolitionist and **philanthropist** from New York. He gave money to various individuals, groups and social justice causes. It is estimated that he donated more than $8 million during his life. That's over £193 million in today's money.

People who supported slavery held their own meetings to share their beliefs. This advert from Arkansas calls for people to "resist the aggressions of the **lawless** abolitionists".

Growing Desperate

Brown grew up in a very religious family who had strong abolitionist beliefs. He married twice and had 20 children.

Not all abolitionists believed in gradually and peacefully freeing enslaved people. Some wanted enslaved people and their allies to rise up and bring about an immediate end to slavery. One of these abolitionists was John Brown.

Brown formed a group of men, some of whom are shown here. After adding five Black men and three of his own sons, he had a group of 22 men. They rented a farm near Harpers Ferry, Virginia, which was a federal **arsenal**.

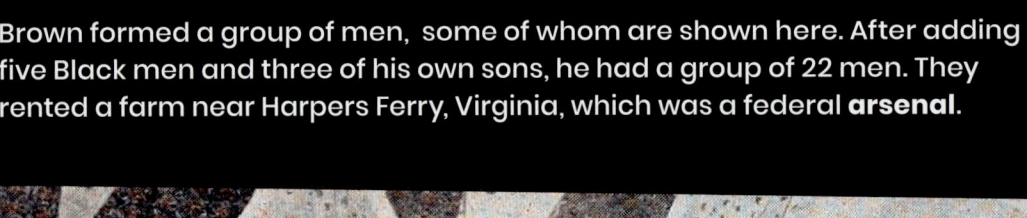

THE SECRET SIX

In 1858, Brown met with six important abolitionists. They were known as the "Secret Six". They planned to give Brown money to help fight slavery. They thought he was going to focus his efforts on Kansas. But Brown wanted to go to Virginia. This made the Secret Six nervous, although they were excited about what might happen.

HARPERS FERRY

Brown's aim was to start an uprising of enslaved people, using weapons from the arsenal. On 16 October 1859, Brown and his men took control of Harpers Ferry. They took hostages and killed five **civilians** in the process. News of their raid spread. On 18 October, Colonel Robert E Lee, Lieutenant JEB Stuart and a company of US Marines surrounded Brown and his men. They ordered Brown to surrender, but he refused. On the morning of 19 October, the soldiers killed 10 of Brown's men, including two of his sons.

This engraving shows Brown being captured.

AFTERMATH

Brown was captured and accused of murder and **treason**. He was tried in court and convicted of all charges. He was executed on 2 December 1859.

Think about it

Despite his violent action, Brown was considered a hero by many people. Why do you think this was?

The Railroad's Impact

The Underground Railroad helped thousands of enslaved people escape to freedom. Although it did not end slavery, it played a critical role in challenging the institution, empowering enslaved individuals and fuelling the abolitionist movement. The movement was so powerful that it became a major reason why Confederate states sought to leave the Union.

THE CIVIL WAR

After President Lincoln's election, South Carolina seceded from the Union in December 1860. This was a sign of the unrest that would follow. From January to June 1861, 10 more southern states seceded. They wanted to keep the institution of slavery, and they were willing to fight for it. Civil war broke out between the North and the South in April 1861. The war centred on issues related to slavery and its expansion into new territories. The outbreak of the war ended the Underground Railroad's operations.

Issued in Washinton, DC on 1 January 1863, the Emancipation Proclamation declared that enslaved people in the states that had seceded were free. It meant that any persons escaping enslavement to states that were part of the Union were permanently free.

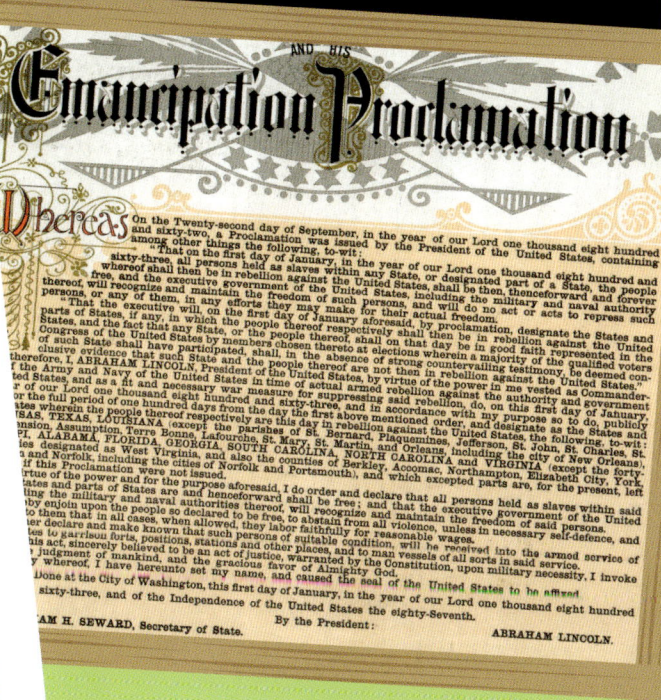

Abraham Lincoln did not want to see slavery expand in the United States, but he also did not call for abolition. This changed during the Civil War, when President Lincoln supported **emancipation** for all enslaved people.

People gathered in Washington, DC to celebrate the abolition of slavery in 1865.

AFTER THE WAR

By the time the war ended and slavery was fully abolished in 1865, about 750,000 American people had been killed. In 1861, this was more than 2 per cent of the population of the US. About 4 million enslaved Black American people were freed. The institution of slavery ended, although **segregation**, racism and **discrimination** did not.

Lessons from History

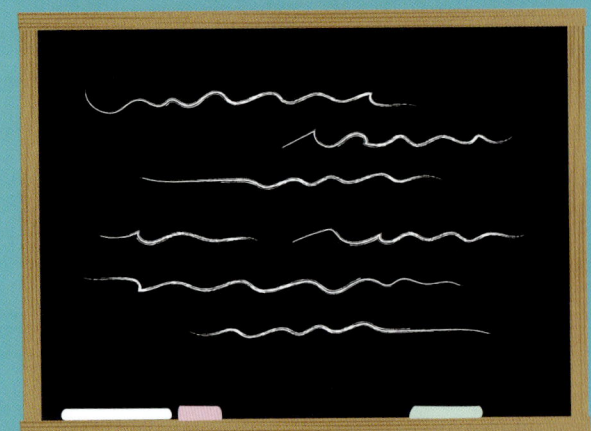

The Underground Railroad was a widespread network of individuals who worked together to help enslaved people find freedom. So why do we remember the Underground Railroad, and what can we learn from it?

UNTOLD STORIES

We know a lot about what happened on the Underground Railroad, largely from stories of those directly affected. Several formerly enslaved people wrote autobiographies, including Sojourner Truth and Frederick Douglass. These accounts allow us to learn about how they found freedom, and about their lives as enslaved people. But we do not know every story. Many people who escaped, or those who helped others, did not talk about it. Some could not read or write. We might never know about what they went through.

Think about it

Do you think we know the full story about the Underground Railroad? Do you think we ever will?

Harriet Tubman with her husband, stepdaughter, extended family and some formerly enslaved people she helped to escape.

HARRIET'S LASTING LEGACY

Harriet Tubman will be remembered as an **integral** part of the Underground Railroad. She showed immense courage as she risked her life to escort people to freedom. During the Civil War, she was a nurse and spy for the Union Army. After the war, she continued to call for equality for Black American people and women.

FROM VILLAINS TO HEROES

At the time of the Underground Railroad, people who helped freedom seekers were breaking the law. The stationmasters, conductors and others working undercover risked their lives to help freedom seekers escape. Now, many of these people are remembered as heroes. This gives us an example of how views can change. It also shows the power of coming together to fight for a cause. The Underground Railroad relied on the teamwork of many individuals.

The Tower Of Freedom in Canada was created by a sculptor called Ed Dwight. It is one of several monuments that help us remember those who were involved in the Underground Railroad, whether we know their stories or not.

A CONTINUED FIGHT

The end of slavery did not put a stop to racial inequality. Some people are still treated unfairly because of their skin colour today. There is still work to do to make sure everyone is treated equally.

This photo is from a Black Lives Matter march in New York City in June 2020. At the march, protestors called for justice after a number of police officers killed Black American individuals, including George Floyd and Breonna Taylor.

Uncovering the Truth

A lot is known about the work of the Underground Railroad and the people it helped. This is because there are so many primary and secondary sources available. A primary source is a document or object created at the time of a historical event. A secondary source is a document or object created after the event, or by someone who was not directly involved in it. They can explain or interpret primary sources. They help in understanding an event.

Primary sources include

- official documents
- letters
- diaries
- paintings or drawings
- photographs
- sound recordings
- videos

Secondary sources include

- news articles
- books
- media documentaries
- encyclopaedias

Photo of original source

DIFFERENT POINTS OF VIEW

Primary and secondary sources may tell different stories depending on the views of the people who created them. A person who agreed with slavery would have a different perspective from an abolitionist. It is important to question sources — doing this helps us to understand them and understand different perspectives better.

RECORD OF FUGITIVES

Although the exact routes of the Underground Railroad are not known, the stories of many freedom seekers are. This photo shows part of a page from Sydney Howard Gay's Record of Fugitives. Gay's office was an Underground Railroad stop and he kept records about the freedom seekers he helped. This is a primary source.

Original source text

April 3rd. Benjn. Moody. + James Cummens, belonged to Col. Jacob Hollingsworth, Hagerstown, Md. left in October.

Stopped all winter at Crosswicks, N.J. with Amos E. Middleton.

Forwarded to Syracuse, paying Benj.'s passage- 3.90

James C. left his mother, Mary Cummens. (Exs _ .25 +his sister Lucy at A. Middleton's.

Benjamin Moody and James Cummens are two of the freedom seekers who were recorded by Gay.

After their escape, they stayed with Amos E Middleton in Crosswicks, New Jersey.

Benjamin and James then went to Syracuse, with Benjamin's travel being paid for.

James left his mother and sister with Amos E Middleton. The notes include some abbreviations that are unclear to modern readers.

Look at the Record of Fugitives, then read the transcribed version of the text and answer the questions below.

Quick questions

- What is the name of the enslaver Benjamin and James escaped from?
- How many freedom seekers are recorded here in total?
- Who paid for Benjamin's travel?

Discussion questions

- Why was it helpful for the station masters to keep a record of people they helped?
- What sources would you look for if you wanted to better understand what it felt like to be a freedom seeker on an Underground Railroad route?

- Jacob Hollingsworth.
- Four: Benjamin Moody, James, Mary and Lucy Cummens.
- The person writing the record (Sydney Howard Gay).

Vocabulary Builder
Secret Journeys

How would the Underground Railroad be reported today? Read this fictional article to see how a newspaper might have covered it at the time. Pay attention to key words that describe the work of the network and how people are responding to it.

THE PATHS TO FREEDOM

The southern states of the US are very angry. Their enslaved workers are finding ways to reach the North to gain their freedom. Plantation owners are blaming Black vigilance committees and white abolitionists for disrupting their lives. It is also believed that some citizens are helping to hide enslaved people in their homes.

Many people in the country have always opposed slavery. At first, Black activists started finding ways to help runaways find freedom. Then white abolitionists started helping the movement.

Abolitionist groups have been speaking out. More and more people are helping freedom seekers move north on secret routes.

In response to the controversy across the country, American people are leaning towards electing Abraham Lincoln as president. While he is not an abolitionist, Lincoln wants to keep slavery contained in the South. Some southern states are threatening to secede from the Union if he wins. American people must decide once and for all if they are for or against the enslavement of their fellow human beings.

Imagine you are writing a report about the work of the Underground Railroad. Then use the article on page 42 and the prompts and word bank below to write your own news story.

- Why was the Underground Railroad needed?
- How did the network help freedom seekers?
- How did views about slavery differ across America?

Describing slavery	injustice, bounty hunter, captivity, discrimination, fugitives, plantation, secrecy, segregation
Working for change	advocate, ally, backing, confrontation, encouragement, opposition, organisation, resistance, solidarity
Actions taken	assist, boycott, conceal, disruption, guide, hide, protect, resist, shelter, support

Glossary

Abolition A movement working to end or stop something, for example, slavery.

Abolitionist Someone who worked to end slavery.

Activist Someone who works for or against an issue or cause.

Advocate Someone who works in support of an issue or cause.

Allies People who help and support other people who are part of a group that is treated badly or unfairly, even though they are not a member of this group.

Amendment A change in a law. In the United States, it is also an official change to the Constitution.

Arsenal A storage place for weapons.

Auction A sale of property to the person who bids the highest or offers the most money.

Bias An attitude that favours one view or position over another.

Bounty A reward offered for the capture of a fugitive.

Bounty hunter A person who tracked down fugitives for reward money.

Boycott The act of not buying or not using something from a company or country to show you disagree with its beliefs, policies or methods. For example, if people do not like how a company treats its workers, they might stop buying its products to force it to change.

Calvinist A very strict group of religious followers who believe that people are predestined to go to heaven or hell.

Captivity Being kept in prison or otherwise not able to leave.

Civil disobedience A form of peaceful protest marked by the refusal to accept certain laws believed to be unjust.

Civilian A person who is not in the military.

Clause A separate part in a formal document.

Condemn To declare something is wrong or unfit.

Congress A body of government in the United States charged with discussing ideas and making decisions. It is made up of the Senate and the House of Representatives.

Constitution The written laws that govern the United States. The United States has separate constitutions for each state, in addition to the United States Constitution that applies to the entire country. Many countries have constitutions.

Crop A plant, such as a grain or vegetable, that is grown for harvest.

Decade A period of ten years.

Delegate A person who represents others at a meeting.

Dictated Speech that is written down.

Discrimination Unfair treatment due to prejudice.

Due process The right to fair treatment in the justice system.

Emancipation To free someone from control or the power of someone else.

Enslaved To be forced to work for someone else without the freedom to stop or leave.

Executed To be put to death as punishment for a crime.

Freedom seeker An enslaved person escaping to freedom.

Fugitive Someone who has run away.

Hackman A cab or carriage driver in the 1700s and 1800s.

Hard labour Very difficult manual work.

Integral To be an essential part of something.

Lawless To not follow any laws.

Legal To be permitted by law.

Liberal Used to describe the belief in individual rights and laws established for the good of the community.

Manifest A list of the cargo and people on a ship.

Mimicked To have copied someone or something.

Minister An official of the Christian church who often leads religious services.

Mortality rate The number of deaths in a specific population during a defined time period (such as a year).

Outlawed When something is made illegal.

Overseer A supervisor or superintendent.

Pamphlet A short, printed publication with no cover.

Petition A written request or demand for change, often including signatures of supporters.

Philanthropist A person who promotes goodwill and gives money to humanitarian causes.

Plantation An estate where profitable crops were grown.

Profitable Something that makes money.

Quaker A member of a religious group known for their values of peace, equality and community.

Ratify To formally approve or sign into law.

Secede To withdraw from a larger unit.

Segregation To be kept separate due to gender, race, religion or other factors.

Slavery A system in which people are owned by their enslavers and forced to work without pay.

Smuggle To export or import secretly and illegally.

Social justice The belief that all people in society deserve social, political and economic equality.

Source A written document, artefact or building that provides information relating to the past. Sources are also known as evidence.

Treason The act of betraying your own country by helping its enemies or by trying to harm it.

Undercover In secret, often while in disguise.

Union A name for the United States, and the name given to the northern states after the southern states had seceded.

Vigilance The state of being watchful in order to avoid danger.

Index

A
abolitionists 8, 13, 21, 32–35, 42
abolition of slavery 37
American Anti-Slavery Society 6
Anti-Slavery Convention of American Women 33
Anti-Slavery Societies 6, 9, 12, 32–33
    Henry "Box" Brown 28
auctions 15
Auld, Sophia 27

B
Black Lives Matter 39
Boston Female Anti-Slavery Society 32
bounty hunters 7, 21, 28, 30
boycotts 6
Brown, Henry "Box" 9, 28
Brown, John 8, 34–35

C
Canada 9, 10–11, 19, 21, 26, 28, 30
    Tower of Freedom 39
capture 30–31
Chapman, Maria Weston 32
civil disobedience 6
Civil War 7, 36–37
Clay, Edward Williams 19
code 26–27
Coffin, Catharine 9, 10–11, 18
Coffin House 10–11, 18
Coffin, Levi 6, 9, 10–11, 18
communication, secret 26–27
conductors 5, 9, 20–21
Cornish, Samuel 13
cotton 14, 15
cotton gin 15
Craft, William and Ellen 9, 29
Cross, John 29

D
Davids, Tice 9, 16
Disappointed Abolitionists, The (Clay) (picture) 19
Dixon, Jeremiah 17
Douglass, Frederick 6, 8, 13, 27, 38
Dwight, Ed 39

E
Emancipation Proclamation 37
engineers 5
enslaved Black Americans 4, 12, 37
    abolitionists 13
    escaped 9, 20, 28–29
    freed 9, 17, 19, 20–21, 37
    life of 14–15
    risk of recapture 30–31

F
Fort Sumter (South Carolina) 7
Foster, Abby Kelley 33
Fountain City (Indiana) 10
freedom seekers 4, 10, 16, 17, 26, 40
    recapture 30
Freedom's Journal (newspapers) 13
Fugitive Slave Acts 7, 29, 30

G
Garrett, Thomas 9, 18
Garrison, William Lloyd 6, 7, 8, 12
Gay, Sydney Howard 40–41
Grant, Ulysses S 7
Grimes, Leonard 9, 20

H
Hamilton, Plat 31
Harpers Ferry (Virginia) 34, 35
Haviland, Laura Smith 21
Hopper, Isaac 17

K
Kentucky 18, 21
kidnappings 31

46

L
Lee, Robert E 7, 35
Liberator, The (newspaper) 6, 7, 8
Liberty Line 29
life expectancy 15
Lincoln, President Abraham 32, 36–37
Loguen, Jermain 9, 19
Lovejoy, Elija 6

M
maps 10–11, 12
Mason, Charles 17
Mason–Dixon Line 17
Missouri Compromise 12
Myers, Stephen 19

N
name, "Underground Railroad" 16
newspapers 6, 7, 8, 13, 29
New York 12, 17, 19, 39
North Star, The (newspaper) 8
Northup, Solomon 9, 31

O
Ohio 11, 13, 18
Ohio River 9, 11, 16, 18
Orleans (ship) 31

P
Parker, John P 21
Pennsylvania 17, 21, 28
philanthropist 33
photography 13
plantations 14, 15
Powers, Harriet 27
punishment 15, 26

Q
Quakers 17, 21
quilts 27

R
racism and racial inequality 37, 39
Rankin, Reverend John and Jean 18
reading 27
rebellions 15
resistance, to abolitionists 33
Ross, Ben 22–25
Ross, Henry 22–25
Ruggles, David 19
Russwurm, John Brown 13

S
Secret Six 34
Smith, Gerrit 33
Smith, Samuel A 28
sources, primary and secondary 40–41
South Carolina 7, 29, 36
stationmasters 5, 9, 18–19
Still, William 22–25
Stuart, JEB 35
survey markers 17

T
Thirteenth Amendment 7
Tower of Freedom (Canada) 39
travel, on the Underground Railroad 4, 16–17
Truth, Sojourner 8, 32, 38
Tubman, Harriet 7, 8, 20, 22–25, 39
    communication and codes 26–27
Tubman, John 22–25
Turner, Nat 15
Twelve Years a Slave (Northup) 31

U
US Constitution 12
    Article Four 30
    Thirteenth Amendment 7

V
vigilance committees 17, 19, 38

W
Western Citizen (newspaper) 29
Whipper, William 9, 21
Whitney, Eli 15

Acknowledgments

The publisher would like to thank the following for their kind permission to reproduce their photographs:

(Key: a-above; b-below/bottom; c-centre; f-far; l-left; r-right; t-top)

4-5 Alamy Stock Photo: Science History Images (t). **4 Alamy Stock Photo:** PAINTING (bl). **6 Alamy Stock Photo:** North Wind Picture Archives (c). **Getty Images:** FPG (cr); mikroman6 (br). **7 Alamy Stock Photo:** ClassicStock (br); Niday Picture Library (tr); IanDagnall Computing (bl). **8 Alamy Stock Photo:** GL Archive (b). **9 Alamy Stock Photo:** Heritage Image Partnership Ltd (tr); Reading Room 202 (cr). **Getty Images:** Heritage Images (br). **10-11 Alamy Stock Photo:** Randy Duchaine (b). **Library of Congress, Washington, D.C.:** Historic American Buildings Survery HABS_IND89_FOUC11 (tc). **10 Alamy Stock Photo:** Stan Rohrer (bl). **11 Indiana State Museum and Historic Sites:** Courtesy of the Indiana State Museum and Historic Sites (br). **12 Alamy Stock Photo:** Alpha Historica (cl); Phil Cardamone (tc). **13 Alamy Stock Photo:** Yogi Black (br); IanDagnall Computing (t). **Bridgeman Images:** The New York Historical (bl). **14 Alamy Stock Photo:** GRANGER - Historical Picture Archive (b); history_docu_photo (tr). **15 Alamy Stock Photo:** Chronicle (br); Heritage Image Partnership Ltd (t); GRANGER - Historical Picture Archive (bc). **16 Alamy Stock Photo:** Photo 12 (t). **Getty Images:** clu (b). **17 Alamy Stock Photo:** Chronicle (tr). **Getty Images:** fotoguy22 (bl). **18 Alamy Stock Photo:** American portraiture (t); Chronicle (bl). **Ohio History Connection:** (br). **19 Alamy Stock Photo:** Historic Collection (t); Science History Images (bl); History and Art Collection (br). **20 Alamy Stock Photo:** Alpha Stock (t); Archive Pics (bl). **21 Alamy Stock Photo:** American portraiture (c); Design Pics Inc (t). **Getty Images:** Fotosearch (b). **26 Alamy Stock Photo:** RTRO (t). **27 Alamy Stock Photo:** Albu (t). **Getty Images:** Fotosearch (b). **28 Getty Images:** MPI (c). **29 Getty Images:** Chicago History Museum (b); Illustrated London News (t); Heritage Images (cr). **30 Alamy Stock Photo:** The Granger Collection. **31 Alamy Stock Photo:** AF Fotografie (br); Classic Image (cl). **The US National Archives and Records Administration:** (tr). **32 Alamy Stock Photo:** GRANGER - Historical Picture Archive (bc); piemags / DCM (t); incamerastock (bl). **33 Alamy Stock Photo:** Imago History Collection (t); The Picture Art Collection (bl). **34 Alamy Stock Photo:** IanDagnall Computing (t); World History Archive (b). **35 Alamy Stock Photo:** Historical Images Archive (t); Niday Picture Library (b). **36 Alamy Stock Photo:** Classic Image. **37 Alamy Stock Photo:** Everett Collection Inc (tl); World History Archive (cr); North Wind Picture Archives (b). **38 Alamy Stock Photo:** The Granger Collection. **39 Alamy Stock Photo:** Alpha Historica (t); NurPhoto SRL (c); Joel Villanueva (b). **40 Columbia Rare Book and Manuscript Library:** (bl). **43 Alamy Stock Photo:** North Wind Picture Archives.

Cover images: *Front:* **Alamy Stock Photo:** history_docu_photo br, PAINTING c, Pictorial Press Ltd t; **Photo Courtesy of Wofford Sculpture Studio, Cambridge, Maryland, © Wesley Wofford**; *Back:* **Alamy Stock Photo:** North Wind Picture Archives t, b; **Indiana State Museum and Historic Sites:** Courtesy of the Indiana State Museum and Historic Sites c.

Quote attributions:

Douglass, Frederick. 1845. *Narrative of the Life of Frederick Douglass, an American Slave.* Boston: Anti-Slavery Office.

All the books in the DK Super History series have been reviewed by authenticity readers to ensure the represented cultures and experiences are accurate.

This book uses language as appropriate to modern contexts. Historical terms that are no longer acceptable may be present in original source materials and images. These sources are included to present authentic insights into history.